Weymouth and Melcombe Regis

in old picture postcards

by
Maureen Boddy
and
Jack West

European Library - Zaltbommel/Netherlands MCMLXXXIV

GB ISBN 90 288 2850 8

European Library in Zaltbommel/Netherlands publishes among other things the following series:

IN OLD PICTURE POSTCARDS *is a series of books which sets out to show what a particular place looked like and what life was like in Victorian and Edwardian times. A book about virtually every town in the United Kingdom is to be published in this series. By the end of this year about 175 different volumes will have appeared. 1,250 books have already been published devoted to the Netherlands with the title* **In oude ansichten.** *In Germany, Austria and Switzerland 500, 60 and 15 books have been published as* **In alten Ansichten;** *in France by the name* **En cartes postales anciennes** *and in Belgium as* **En cartes postales anciennes** *and/or* **In oude prentkaarten** *150 respectively 400 volumes have been published.*

For further particulars about published or forthcoming books, apply to your bookseller or direct to the publisher.

This edition has been printed and bound by Grafisch Bedrijf De Steigerpoort in Zaltbommel/Netherlands.

INTRODUCTION

The invention of the camera, followed by the introduction of the picture postcard during the closing years of the nineteenth century combined to produce a virtual flood of illustrations of local scenes. Holiday resorts such as Weymouth have been particularly well recorded, and this collection has been brought together in an effort to present a picture of the town during the years 1870 to 1930. All the pictures in the collection were taken during this period, but it is difficult to consider events in isolation, and the notes accompanying each view endeavour to describe the changes which have taken place before and since the scenes were recorded.

Included in the collection are pictures of communities which did not in fact become part of Weymouth until 1933, when the Borough boundaries were extended to include the parishes of Broadwey, Radipole, Preston and Sutton Poyntz, Upwey and Wyke Regis. The town of Weymouth had long been the focal point for this group of villages, and the general growth of housing during the period following the First World War had resulted in 'Weymouth' moving out to meet its smaller neighbours. The eventual enlargement of the Borough boundaries was a logical step.

These villages are of far more ancient origin than either of the two rival ports which developed at the mouth of the River Wey. The original 'Weymouth', on the south side of the harbour, was almost certainly settled by men from Wyke, and was in fact part of the Parish of Wyke Regis until 1837. Similarly, Melcombe Regis on the north shore was part of Radipole Parish until 1606. Forced to share the profits from the narrow river-mouth harbour, a rivalry developed and continued for centuries, during which period they both achieved independent borough status. The bitterness between them only ceased after their enforced union by Royal Charter in 1571.

Officially The Borough of Weymouth and Melcombe Regis, the combined town became known merely as Weymouth, the harbour remaining its main source of income, although trade was greatly diminished following disastrous Civil War fighting in the 1640's. A general revival in the prosperity of the town did not occur until the mid-eighteenth century, when doctors began to recommend sea bathing as a new cure for all ills. To set the seal on Weymouth's new prosperity as a health and pleasure resort, King George III made the town his summer home during the years 1789-1805 and many of the buildings shown in these illustrations date from the days of 'Royal Weymouth'. For a brief period it was the most fashionable place in England.

In those years only the wealthy and privileged could afford long holidays by the sea, but by the time the first of these photographs was taken the railway had reached Weymouth and the character of the resort was changing. A good train service, cheap fares and the introduction of statutory Bank Holidays led to hundreds of ordinary people visiting the seaside and the genteel resort of Georgian times was required to accommodate them in lodgings much less expensive than those rented by the nobility and gentry at the beginning of the century.

At the same time as the fortunes of Weymouth improved with its establishment as a seaside resort, the harbour entered on a new lease of life with the build up of regular trade with the Channel Islands. The fortunes of the harbour from the days when the Great Western Railway took over the Weymouth-Channel Islands service in the late 1880's can be followed, and in many of the harbour pictures can be seen the paddle steamers of Cosens' fleet, those little ships which were to provide pleasure trips for thousands of visitors for more than a century.

The photographs also show the many changes which the seaside itself underwent in a sixty year period, most noticeable on the beach, where costume and entertainment so readily assist in dating the pictures of a bygone age. Bathing machines, still in active use at the end of the period, now seem as outdated as the horse-drawn waggonettes which once plied for hire on the Esplanade. The building developments are clearly shown too, as the town spread out on to land reclaimed from both the sea and the Backwater.

There are reminders of the effects of war on Weymouth. Not only can they be seen in the early views of streets and buildings since destroyed during Second World War air raids, but also in the many projects which were to provide work for the unemployed during the depression which followed the First World War. These included two bridges (Westham Bridge of 1921, and the Town Bridge of 1930), extensions to the Esplanade, public gardens laid out in several parts of the town, and extensive reclamation works.

No town can stand still, and the majority of the scenes have been included because they reveal just how much the town has altered over the years. In just a few cases however, a postcard has been included because it shows that in an age of change there can be continuity, and that it is possible for a scene to be instantly recognised and yet clearly belong to another age.

For permission to use pictures from the collections at Weymouth Library and Weymouth Museum our grateful thanks are due to Mr. H.E. Radford, F.L.A., Dorset County Librarian, and Mr. M. Ridley, Curator, respectively. Our thanks also to Mrs. B. Cornick for the loan of a family photograph and to Mr. Terry Gale for permission to use postcards from his collection.

1. One of the earliest aerial photographs of Weymouth, dating from 1912, when aeroplanes were still a novelty. On the far (southern) side of the harbour stand 'old' Weymouth and the Chapelhay, much of which was destroyed during the air raids of the Second World War. Two cross-channel steamers are tied up in The Cove, another is alongside the cargo stage, whilst a number of Cosens' paddle-steamers are secured to various harbour quays. The bandstand in the gardens was converted to The Kursaal in 1913, but then completely replaced by the Alexandra Gardens Theatre in 1924. St. Mary's Church, parish church of Melcombe Regis and the largest building in the centre foreground, backs onto a crowded group of small houses which occupied the site of a mediaeval priory. These were cleared away during the 1960's to form a car park.

2. Linking the ancient town of Weymouth (on the far side) and Melcombe Regis (where the photographer was standing) has been a succession of bridges, all but one of which stood on this site. The Town Bridge shown here was the first to be built of stone and was erected in 1824. It was partly rebuilt in 1881 when it was fitted with the single swing opening section, thus continuing to permit the passage of ships up harbour. When the photograph was taken in mid-1928, work was already in hand on its replacement, and by the end of the year the bridge had been totally demolished. Two years later the present-day bridge was opened in its place. Apart from Holy Trinity Church, the skyline has altered completely and is formed today by large blocks of flats and other housing, many of the buildings shown here have been badly hit during Second World War air raids.

3. Buildings on the left-hand side of this photograph have altered very little since this view was taken in 1928, but on the opposite side of the approach to the Town Bridge, the large block of Georgian houses and shops was shortly to be demolished to improve the approach to the new bridge. The open stalls on the small triangle of road beneath the advertisement for the 'Regent Cinema' are a link with the old market which operated in this general area prior to the opening of the Market House in St. Mary Street in 1855. The bell turret standing against the open sky belonged to Holy Trinity Schools, erected in 1853 and damaged by bombs during the Second World War.

4. June 1930 and the paddlesteamer *Monarch* receives attention whilst final work is in progress for the completion of the new Town Bridge. Stands for the official opening are being erected on the site of the former Georgian houses and shops, whilst a steam roller and road gang prepare the surface of the approach-ramp from St. Thomas Street. Trinity Road, on the far side of the harbour, at one time formed part of High Street, and retains some of its Georgian and much of its Victorian character. The line where the new bridge divides in the centre into separate lifting halves, shows clearly as the result of contrasting road surfaces.

5. The descent from the Town Bridge to St. Thomas Street and the main town shopping centre is the setting for this 1905 view. One of the earliest motor-buses in this area, a Great Western Railway vehicle en route from Radipole to Wyke Regis, prepares to face the climb over the bridge, whilst a horse-drawn 'hotel bus' delivers passengers from the railway station to the Crown Hotel. The Crown Hotel has since enlarged its premises by taking in the adjoining property, but on the opposite side of the road, the imposing corner shop of 'Strong and Williams' was demolished in 1937 as the first stage of a scheme of road widening which was intended to eventually include the adjacent shops in St. Thomas Street. Recent building developments on these adjoining sites show that the modern one-way traffic system no longer calls for a general widening of the street at this point.

6. The new General Post Office on the corner of St. Thomas Street and Lower St. Alban Street had been completed in 1907, prior to which the Royal Mail had been handled from premises nearer to the Town Bridge. Although of imposing external appearance, it was not large enough and complaints of delays and overcrowding began almost from the time it opened. By 1911 the Post Office had purchased the adjoining property with a view to expansion, but it was to be 1921 before work began on extending the premises. The addition to the General Post Office in St. Thomas Street was completed in 1922 and carried out in a style which matched the original to a degree which makes it difficult today to distinguish between the original building and the extension. This postcard also gives a glimpse of the building on the opposite corner of Lower Bond Street, now demolished and replaced by Tesco.

7. The Georgian origins of much of the property shown in this 1910 postcard of St. Thomas Street reflect an earlier period of the town's history. It is unlikely that many of the buildings were designed with shop-fronts, although they accept the additions shown here with rather better grace than they do the more spectacular conversions of the later twentieth century. The shop in the left-hand corner of the picture was demolished and rebuilt as an extension to the main Post Office in 1921. The carrier's cart ambles along the centre of what is today the busiest street in the town centre, with traffic flowing in one direction only, towards the viewer.

8. In 1890 Vilat Hackfath Bennett opened his large store on the corner of St. Thomas Street and Middle Bond Street, and this postcard of the early years of this century shows the premises as originally designed. Large brass signs above the shopfront informed the public that Mr. Bennett was a 'Draper and Mercer', i.e. a retailer of textile fabrics, including silk, but over the years the range of goods extended and this became Weymouth's principal departmental store. The premises were enlarged in 1923 by the addition of the adjoining property, which in this view was owned by Rendell and Sons, Painters and Decorators. Eventually acquired by the Debenham group, the store closed in 1982, and has since been rebuilt internally. On the left can be seen the offices of the Weymouth Waterworks Company, later to move to Mitchell Street.

9. Once known as 'Gregory's Corner', this block stood at the junction of St. Thomas Street and Lower Bond Street. Local chemist Gregory occupied this site, Nos. 75 and 76 St. Thomas Street, from the middle of the nineteenth century until the early 1900's. Eventually Mr. Gregory sold part of his premises for re-development, enabling the Devon and Cornwall Bank to build a new office on the corner site. Lloyds Bank sign next appeared in front of No. 76, following its amalgamation with the Devon and Cornwall, and when in 1914 Lloyds moved to premises at No. 92 St. Mary Street, the National Provincial Bank moved here. The bank and chemist continued side by side until the mid 1960's when Gregorys closed and No. 75 was converted for use by the bank. Following further amalgamations, the name has once again changed to the National Westminster Bank.

10. Parallel to St. Thomas Street runs the equally ancient thoroughfare of St. Nicholas Street, and here in 1907 was erected the Sailors' Home. The steady increase in the number and size of Royal Naval ships operating in local waters had resulted in hundreds of sailors being on shore leave in the town and a constant demand for suitable overnight accommodation. The premises were opened in February 1907. One commentator described the new home as 'Weymouth's most distinguished building of the past hundred years', but, because of the narrow streets in this part of the town, it could never be seen to full advantage. Renamed The White Ensign Club, its use declined with the reduction in the manning of Naval vessels, and it was demolished in October, 1970. A building of very specialised design, it had proved impracticable to convert for other uses, and the site was later used for the construction of a super-market.

11. The Weymouth Royal Hospital and Dispensary was opened in School Street in 1872, having previously occupied a number of different premises in the town since its inception in 1816. In 1921 it combined with the Princess Christian Hospital at Greenhill to form the Weymouth and District Hospital, and the School Street premises were sold to the Salvation Army. For almost another sixty years it continued to provide a valued service as a 'hostel' until rising costs forced the Salvation Army to close the premises and dispose of the site. A new shopping precinct has been erected in its place and, known as The Colwell Shopping Centre, it perpetuates the name of one of the most respected local Salvation Army leaders.

12. Dating from 1890 this view of Weymouth seafront was taken just a year before the demolition of the bow-windowed Royal Hotel in the centre of the photograph. This was the building which had housed the Assembly Rooms, meeting place of fashionable society during the period of the visits to Weymouth of King George III. Cabmen wait for fares beside the Cabmen's Shelter, now better known as the Tea Cabin. The newest Victorian attraction on the Esplanade is also shown – the Jubilee Clock, erected opposite the end of King Street to commemorate Queen Victoria's Golden Jubilee of 1887, and still a prominent landmark today.

13. The original Royal Hotel, one of the first buildings erected especially to accommodate the growing numbers of visitors who were coming to Weymouth to experience the new fashion of sea bathing, was built in the 1770's. It stood on the same site as the present Royal Hotel, but this was then an isolated position north of the town. As the holiday industry expanded it set the pattern for the buildings which followed along the Esplanade, as the town turned round to face the sea, its new source of income. Prior to the development of the seaside the houses of the town had clustered around the harbour. The Royal Hotel was pulled down in 1891, having proved too small for the expanding Victorian resort.

14. For a few years in the 1890's there was a large vacant site on Weymouth Esplanade following the demolition of the Georgian Royal Hotel. On the sands three different types of bathing machines can be seen. In the background are the octagonal machines dating from the days of 'Royal Weymouth'. Only one of these – believed to be the machine used by King George III – has survived, and, restored, is on display in Weymouth Museum. Victorian bathing machines are grouped in the centre, and on the far right are the large bathing saloons. Along with a cubicle, bathing drawers could also be hired, and these can be seen flapping in the breeze outside the saloons!

15. Taken in 1923, the central feature of this photograph is the twin-towered Royal Hotel of 1897, its elaborate late-Victorian style of architecture contrasting with that of the more dignified terraces built by the Georgians a hundred years before. Moving south, the other large building with a roof line higher than its neighbour is the Victorian wing added to the Gloucester Hotel in the 1860's to house the exclusive County Club. Note the extension to Weymouth Esplanade around the Jubilee Clock – work carried out in the 1920's to provide a wider promenade for the visitors who thronged the seafront in the summer months, and at the same time, to prevent the pebbles at the northern end of the beach from encroaching on Weymouth's star attraction – its wide golden sands.

16. Coronation Year, 1911, saw the erection of this splendid temporary archway spanning the Esplanade at the end of King Street. Bedecked with greenery, flowers and flags, it was surmounted by a representation of the ship on the Weymouth and Melcombe Regis coat of arms. The elaborate arch commemorated two important events. In this picture it is welcoming visitors to the Royal Counties Agricultural Show, a very prestigious event held on land off the Dorchester Road, adjoining Lodmoor, on June 13th-16th. The mottoes on the arch were then replaced by new lettering proclaiming 'God Bless Our King and Queen' in celebration of the Coronation Day of King George V and Queen Mary on 22nd June 1911. Note the fairy lights along the Esplanade, to be replaced by electric light illuminations later that summer.

17. The central feature of Weymouth Esplanade is the Jubilee Clock, seen here standing on its original stone and concrete platform which was built out on to Weymouth beach. This base disappeared in the 1920's beneath the large extension of the Esplanade seaward around the clock, which today stands on the edge of the roadway. The Jubilee Clock was the town's tribute to the fiftieth year of the reign of Queen Victoria in 1887, although another year elapsed before it was completed. Beyond the clock can be seen one of the attractive cast-iron shelters of the same decade, some of which have remained in use for almost 100 years. The figure printed at the base of the card is a reference number and not the date, which is about 1905.

The Clock Tower, Weymouth. 1941.

18. The Jubilee Clock in the 1920's, illustrating how its original small plinth has been lost beneath the Esplanade extension of 1922. The contrast between this view and the previous photograph can lead to the erroneous belief that the clock tower was actually moved from its original site, but it has in fact always stood on the same spot. Sir Henry Edwards, whose statue stands outside the Alexandra Gardens, donated the original works of the clock, whilst the cost of the tower was raised by public subscription. The illuminated dial was originally gas-lit, but today both this and the clock mechanism are electrically operated.

19. Outdoor band concerts were a popular entertainment in Victorian and Edwardian times, and continued until well into the twentieth century. In 1907 Weymouth erected this second seafront bandstand, the first having been the central feature of the Alexandra Gardens, at the opposite end of the Esplanade, since 1891. The newer bandstand stood opposite Victoria Terrace, and Brunswick Terrace can be seen in the background of this postcard view. The attractive structure stood on the shingle until the promenade was widened around it in 1924. Before this date crowds congregating to listen to the music caused congestion on this narrow walkway, as shown here. The bandstand disappeared late in the 1930's, when it was removed to make way for the present Pier Bandstand, a larger entertainment centre in the same area, but built out into the bay on a pile-supported structure.

20. This was the last of the cast-iron and glass seafront shelters erected late in Queen Victoria's reign, and it stood opposite Brunswick Terrace. The terrace, originally known as Brunswick Buildings, was completed in 1827 and remains largely unaltered today. Touches of filigree cast-iron work added an attractive finish to the street furniture – seen here decorating the seafront shelter and street lamp. The lamp post has been replaced by modern street lighting, and the shelter no longer stands outside the houses of Brunswick Terrace. This photograph dates from about 1910.

21. The public gardens at Greenhill were laid out in the 1870's on land belonging to Sir Frederic Johnstone. This Edwardian view shows gravelled walks bordered by high hedges – today the gardens are filled with flowers, including Weymouth's Floral Clock. A feature of the gardens since 1952 is a weathervane commemorating the establishment of a world air speed record of 406.92 mph on 29th September 1931 when Flight-Lieutenant G.H. Stainforth, A.F.C. was a member of the Schneider Trophy team. Flight-Lieutenant Stainforth was an old boy of Weymouth College and the weathervane was previously erected over the college. When the public school closed, shortly after the outbreak of the Second World War, the weathervane, in the form of a seaplane, was presented to the town. The gardens have been much extended during this century and now include putting and bowling greens, tennis courts and beach chalets.

22. Weymouth had been much enhanced in the latter half of the nineteenth century by the laying-out of public gardens at both ends of the Esplanade (the Alexandra Gardens and Greenhill Gardens) and the less formal arrangement of walks on the Nothe headland. In 1904, just off the Dorchester Road, St. John's Gardens were opened opposite the church. This quiet, attractive spot was in an area which had developed rapidly in the late-Victorian period as large villas were built on both sides of the main road. The gardens were on land presented by Sir Frederic Johnstone and were opened by the Mayoress of Weymouth on 20th July 1904. The town's larger gardens along Radipole Park Drive are of much later date and are laid out on land reclaimed from the Backwater in the 1920's.

23. The left-hand side of this photograph of Dorchester Road shows Weymouth College, the boys public school which had transferred to this new site in 1865, having been founded two years earlier in the building which now houses Weymouth Arts Centre in Commercial Road. Originally known as Weymouth Grammar School, the name changed a few years later to Weymouth Collegiate School, eventually becoming known as Weymouth College. The buildings were extended over the years, and this picture must date from about 1880, certainly before the college chapel was built in 1896. In the background, in front of St. John's Church, can be seen old farm buildings on what is today the corner of Carlton Road. Weymouth College closed during the Second World War and its scholars were transferred to Wellingborough, Northamptonshire.

24. The donkeys on Weymouth sands have been a feature of the resort since Victorian times and have always been owned and managed by one family – the Downtons. In this scene from the early 1900's, large Bathing Saloons can be seen on the left of the picture. The hire of a cubicle in the Ladies or Gentlemen's Saloons was cheaper than the hire of an individual machine. The original individual machines, many of which survived from the Georgian period, were all sold during the First World War, and when new machines were provided during the early 1920's they were no longer designed to be towed out into the water. All machines, including the larger saloons, were removed from the beach during the Second World War and did not reappear when hostilities ended. Today, Mr. John Downton's donkey rides operate from a point slightly to the south of the pitch shown here.

25. On a wet and windy Christmas-Day morning in 1930, residents along the Esplanade awoke to the unusual sight of a shipwreck on Weymouth sands. The French ketch *L'Arguenon* had dragged her anchors in the night and was aground on the beach by morning. The ketch, in ballast, was bound from Poole to St. Malo. Those of her crew who remained on board enjoyed a parcel of Christmas fare and provisions, but their attempts to get the ketch off the sands on Boxing-Day failed. Naval men in a steam pinnace were also forced to abandon their salvage efforts. Hopes of refloating *L'Arguenon* were fading until, lightened of ballast and in favourable conditions of wind and tide, she was got off by Mr. Louis Basso, a well-known salvage expert in the Weymouth/Portland area.

26. Children of the 1920's enjoying donkey rides on Weymouth sands, by which time other entertainments have appeared on the beach, including swings and the open-air Vaudeville Theatre. This concert platform, in the centre background of the photograph, provided a summer stage for the concert parties and pierrots who toured the resorts. On the slope leading down to the sands can be seen one of the more unusual forms of transport available in the years before the Second World War – carts drawn by goats. Children sat in these delightful wicker-work creations to be taken up and down the Esplanade, or on short trips around the town. One cart survived the war and continued in use until the 1950's.

27. 'Yeomanry Week' at Weymouth, was an event much enjoyed by the inhabitants, for the arrival in the town of the Queen's Own Dorset Yeomanry Cavalry on their annual spell of permanent drill brought colour, spectacle and entertainment. Heavy rain during the 1898 visit had thinned the crowds when this photograph was taken, as the Yeomanry in splendid uniforms of blue, scarlet and white made their way past the Gloucester Hotel. Military exercises, shooting contests and parades alternated with events such as tug-of-war competitions, concerts and horse and pony races on the sands. The houses adjoining the Gloucester Hotel still possessed front gardens!

28. King George III and members of the Royal Family stayed at Gloucester Lodge almost every year between 1789 and 1805. Their summer home, and the central feature of this photograph, had been built by the King's younger brother, William Henry, Duke of Gloucester, in about 1780. The large extension on the left is an addition of the 1860's, the Lodge having been sold by its Royal owners in 1820 and in later years converted to a hotel. In Georgian times gardens known as The Shrubbery stretched south from Gloucester Lodge right down to the town. Royal visitors entered the Lodge from these gardens through an entrance in the side of the building. The front entrance, shown here, is one of the alterations made since its conversion to an hotel.

29. On 3rd March 1927 the Gloucester Hotel caught fire and this photograph shows the scene shortly after the Weymouth Fire Brigade had extinguished the blaze. Although the roof was destroyed and there was a great deal of damage inside the building, the Georgian façade was almost untouched. After the fire, rebuilding provided the opportunity to extend the former Royal Lodge and an extra storey was added, together with a second floor of attic bedrooms in the roof. The additions were in keeping with the original architectural style of the building, thus retaining its Georgian appearance. The present veranda which runs the entire length of the hotel was erected in the 1970's, replacing an earlier version.

30. Waggonettes line up at the King's Statue ready to take visitors to the local beauty spots – the advertisement on the right offers a trip to Sutton Poyntz and the Osmington White Horse for 1s.3d. (6½p). The photograph probably dates from the early 1900's, certainly before 1905 when the firm of booksellers W.H. Smith arrived in Weymouth and altered the ground floor of the imposing round house at the top of St. Thomas Street. On the right can be seen the very narrow entrance to Westham Road, then known as Little George Street. Here, the end house of Royal Terrace was demolished in 1929 to provide better access at this junction. On the opposite corner the ground floor of the last building in Frederick Place has been much changed and is now Forte's Restaurant. The shops visible on the extreme left of the picture are in St. Mary Street.

31. The King's Statue, as drawn by Robert J. Smart, art master at Weymouth Grammar School in the 1920's and 1930's. He published a series of Weymouth drawings as picture postcards and this view shows the details of the two Georgian roundhouses which form the entrance to the town's main streets, St. Mary Street and St. Thomas Street. Statue House, on the left, remains largely unaltered today, but its companion has undergone a change of shopfront at street level since this drawing was made. At this time the statue was enclosed by Victorian railings, but in the 1950's the Statue Gardens were laid out as part of a large traffic island which now surrounds the Royal monument.

32. In 1897, the sixtieth anniversary of Queen Victoria's accession to the throne was the occasion for great celebrations at Weymouth and the crowds have turned out to hear the customary Loyal Address read by the Mayor at the King's Statue. A salute from the guns at the Nothe Fort was followed by a civic procession through the town, a service at St. Mary's Church, entertainments for young and old and the illumination of the town and seafront in the evening. The statue is bedecked with flags and lamps for the great day and two intrepid Weymouthians have joined King George III on top of the pedestal to enjoy a better view of the borough's tribute to his grand-daughter's Diamond Jubilee.

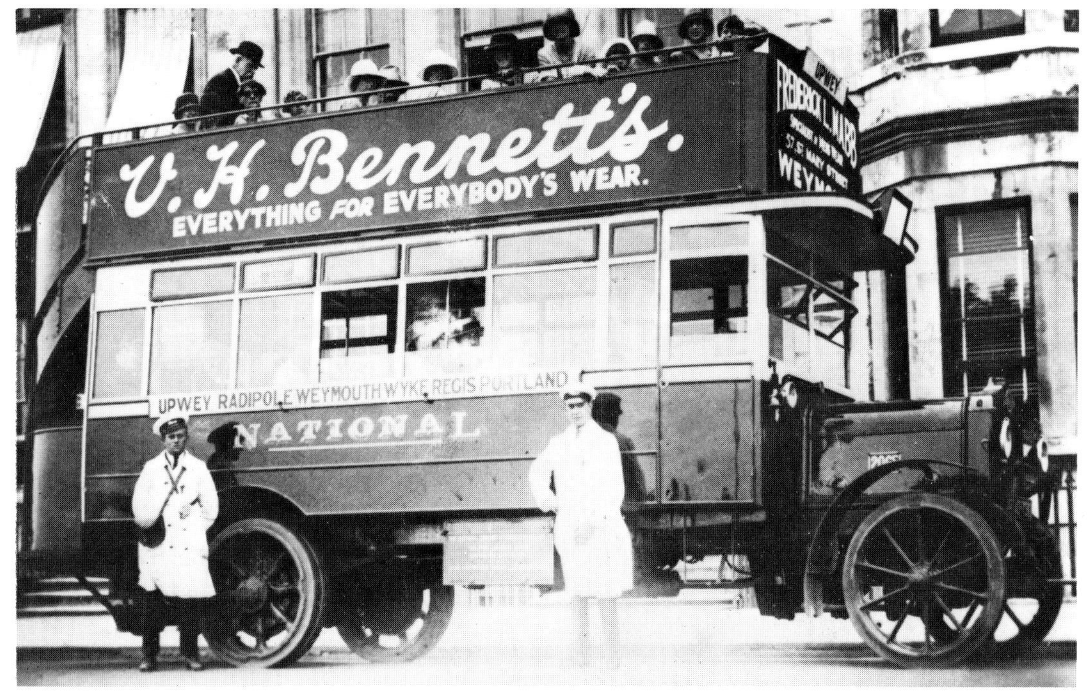

33. The Great Western Railway had first used buses in Weymouth as early as 1905, but the years following the First World War saw a rapid expansion in the provision of independent local bus services. The pioneers in this field were largely Weymouth men, but in 1923 two larger firms began operating in the South Dorset area, The Road Motors Ltd., of Luton, and The National Omnibus Company. Eventually the National Company was to buy out its main rival, The Road Motors, and the numerous local operators, and this old postcard shows an early 'National' bus as used on the Portland-Weymouth-Upwey service.

34. Late in 1867, a wealthy visitor to Weymouth, Mr. George Robert Stephenson, purchased an area of land at the southern end of the Esplanade and then called The Rings, to be laid out as public gardens. Known for some years as The New Gardens, it was decided in 1880 to name them the Alexandra Gardens. They were further enhanced in 1891 by the erection of a bandstand and in 1904 by the addition of a number of attractive thatched shelters. The terraces of Georgian houses in the background, Devonshire and Pulteney Buildings (now Nos. 1-15 The Esplanade), date from the early years of the nineteenth century. Bank Buildings, the terrace on the right, takes its name from the Weymouth and Dorsetshire Bank which occupied the building shown here as the Marine Family Hotel. This became the Edward Hotel in 1913, and is now converted into apartments.

35. The Alexandra Gardens bandstand festooned with electric lights, fairy lamps and lanterns, providing a delightful setting for evening concerts performed by Herr Meier's famous orchestra in 1911 – a most successful season according to the local press. Electric lights were first used to illuminate the Esplanade in August of that year, celebrating the Royal Dorset Yacht Club's Coronation Regatta. Sacred, popular and military music concerts all featured in the Gardens. At the height of the summer audiences were estimated to number over 1,000, and Saturday concerts here were enlivened by firework displays.

36. In 1913 it was decided to provide audiences who gathered in the Alexandra Gardens with additional shelter to enable them to enjoy band concerts during inclement weather. This glass structure was erected around the original bandstand, the roof of which can be seen in the centre of the new 'Kursaal', a name taken from similar buildings in the German health resorts. The Kursaal lasted only a little over ten years, and for part of that time it was used as a reception centre for Australian troops who were in camps around the town during the First World War.

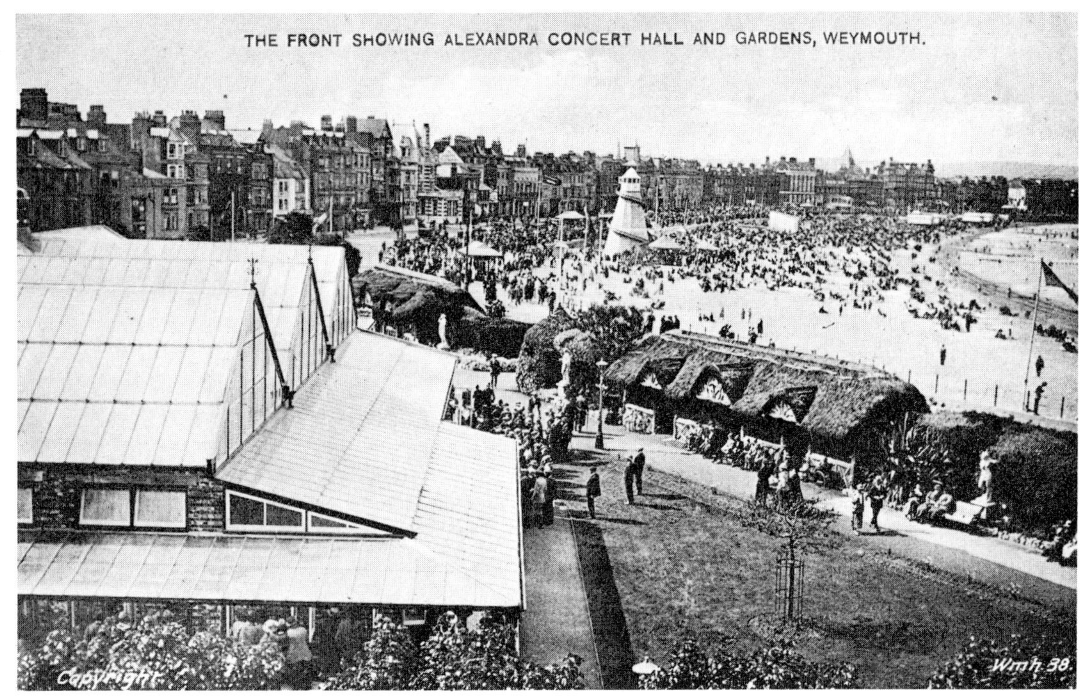

37. This postcard was probably published shortly after the opening of the Alexandra Gardens Theatre in 1924. Known in its early days as the Alexandra Concert Hall, the new building replaced the glass Kursaal and the original bandstand was transferred to the Nothe Gardens. The Alexandra Gardens have changed greatly in recent years. All the thatched shelters have disappeared and the theatre itself lost popularity when the present Pavilion was opened in 1960. It was converted into an amusement centre, and the lawns which surrounded it have given way to children's rides and similar attractions. Just outside the Gardens stands a statue of Sir Henry Edwards, Victorian M.P. for the town, whose generosity did much to improve the lot of the local poor. The helter-skelter appeared on the beach for a short time in the mid-1920's, having previously stood on the shore of Radipole Lake.

38. The original Pavilion Theatre, built on reclaimed land on the Weymouth Bay side of Weymouth Pier, was opened in December 1908. A very attractive example of 'seaside architecture', the Pavilion was built largely of wood and had an outdoor balcony to enable its patrons to enjoy sea views. Part of the building was requisitioned for military use in the First World War and the entire building was taken over during the Second World War. It remained in the control of the War Office until 1947, being used as a Naval Post Office following the peace of 1945. The theatre re-opened in the early 1950's, taking a new name – The Ritz. Its new lease of life was short lived however, for the building was devastated by fire in 1954. The present Pavilion opened in 1960 on the same site. The ornamental pier toll house to the right of the picture was demolished later the same year to improve the approaches to the new theatre.

39. The interior of Weymouth's original Pavilion Theatre, decorated in opulent Edwardian style. Shades of ivory, cream, gold and deep pink were used, with crimson for the curtaining and the tip-up seats. Seating over 1,000 people, the building was opened just before Christmas 1908 by the Earl of Shaftesbury, who unlocked the door with a golden key enamelled with the Borough coat of arms. Here, in the theatre's early days, touring companies presented programmes which changed twice weekly. Tea dances could be enjoyed in the Royal Palm Court extension at the rear of the building. In later years films were to become a regular feature at the Pavilion. The theatre closed during the Second World War, having been requisitioned by the military. Fire claimed the entire wooden structure in 1954 only a short time after its successful re-opening as The Ritz.

40. In 1909 roller skating was all the rage and although there were facilities for indoor skating at the Jubilee Hall, there was a great demand for another skating rink. This the Corporation provided on the Pier, at the rear of the Pavilion Theatre. On payment of a 2d. admission fee, in addition to the usual 2d. pier toll, skaters could enjoy 1,500 square yards of asphalted surface, including a straight run of 200 feet. A second outdoor rink opened at the Jubilee Hall and both must have been welcomed by strollers on the Esplanade who had been much inconvenienced by devotees of the new craze whizzing past them on roller skates. In 1910 the area at the rear of the Pavilion was enclosed, providing an indoor rink on the site, later to become the Royal Palm Court Dance Hall when the skating craze died.

41. Palm trees outside the Pavilion Theatre form a partial frame-work for this view of the southern end of the Esplanade in 1929. The trees have long since gone, but others have been successfully planted along the length of the promenade. The Skee Ball Pavilion of the 1920's alongside the Alexandra Gardens was never a thing of beauty, but it was an accepted feature of the holiday scene. Apart from the demolition of this small amusement centre after the Second World War, little has changed in the general appearance of the Esplanade buildings, other than the modernisation of some of the shopfronts. The roundabout shown here is now lost beneath the wide piazza which fronts the modern Weymouth Pavilion, whilst the Clark and Endicott Memorial, on the right, first erected here in 1914, has found a new home in the Alexandra Gardens.

42. This view of Devonshire Buildings dates from about 1885, at which date the railway along Weymouth Quay ended at this point. As originally constructed, this terrace had a square end, but in 1819, Mr. Welsford, the owner, agreed to take down the last house and reconstruct it with a round end, thus matching similar terraces near the King's Statue. Clarence Buildings, the terrace on the right-hand side of the view and facing the camera, marks the approximate limit of the original shoreline. All land seaward of that line has been reclaimed from the sea since the seventeenth century, thus extending the harbour facilities, and providing land on which these final Esplanade terraces were built.

43. A few years later than the previous postcard, this shows Devonshire Buildings from the harbour, with the Great Western Railway steamer *Ibex* secured alongside the cargo stage. The sailing vessel is the *May* of Rochester, a typical sailing barge which traded in and out of the port of Weymouth, bringing cement from the Medway and the Isle of Wight, and often returning with loads of Portland stone. These barges also crossed to the Channel Islands and were regular visitors to the port until the 1930's. The normal crew was two men and a boy, and they provided an economical if somewhat slow means of transporting bulk goods.

44. Whilst Cosens paddle steamer *Brodick Castle* collects its quota of passengers from Weymouth Pier about 1890, a Great Western Railway cross-channel vessel enters the port of Weymouth on its return from the Channel Islands. A second paddle steamer has been hauled up on the slipway at the very right of the picture, whilst yet another is moored alongside at the foot of the ramp. This slipway was one of the main 'servicing areas' for the local fleet of paddle steamers throughout the whole of the period during which they were a feature of seaside Weymouth. Today, the portion of Weymouth pier shown at the left of the view is occupied by the roll-on-roll-off facilities of the modern port of Weymouth. The extended pier, partly of solid construction and partly built on wooden piles, had been completed in 1860, and apart from the addition of the passenger landing stage in 1889, remained largely unaltered until it was completely rebuilt in 1933.

45. Largest of the paddle steamers operated by Cosens and Co. and pride of the local fleet was the *Majestic*. At 408 tons gross, it was more than twice the size of the majority of the local pleasure steamers, and operated mainly from Bournemouth during the years 1901 to 1914, offering some of the longest day excursions ever provided by the company. Requisitioned for war service, it was converted to a minesweeper and was sunk in the Mediterranean Sea on 28th July 1916. This postcard is one of a series published by Cosens and Co. depicting the local 'paddlers' during the years prior to the First World War.

46. The Nothe Walk has been a feature of Weymouth harbourside since the 1870's, when the Nothe Fort was completed and consideration given to the laying out of the headland for the benefit of local residents and visitors. Formerly the ballast wharf, the scenic details have changed little since this view was taken about 1905; what has altered is the style of dress of the young children, and the size and design of the yachts moored alongside. This was once a favourite mooring for the large and luxurious steam yachts which visited the port during the summer season, whereas today it is the home of many of the smaller sailing yachts which make Weymouth their headquarters.

47. The Nothe Gardens on a warm summer afternoon in the late 1920's. The bandstand which is such a prominent feature was moved here from the Alexandra Gardens in 1924, and survived in its new location for another forty years. The Nothe headland has been a traditional playground for the people of Weymouth for countless generations and lengthy negotiations over the rights of residents took place at the time of building the Nothe Fort in the 1860's. The gardens were eventually laid out in 1888-89, with major improvements in 1909. They look out across Newton's Cove, an area which has been considered for commercial development on more than one occasion but which still retains much of its natural charm.

48. The headland overlooking the mouth of Weymouth Harbour has been the site of a fortification or gun emplacement from the earliest times, but the large stone fort of today dates only from the Victorian period. Designed as part of the fortifications for Portland Harbour, it was built during the 1860's as a casemated fort, with ten heavy guns facing seawards and two smaller ones facing inland. Many of these gun emplacements were later obscured by the great earthen embankment added to the top of the sea wall, and clearly shown in this view dating from the early 1920's. The fort is no longer owned by the military, and is one of Weymouth's showplaces. Fishing from the Stone Pier has always been a pastime for both visitors and residents alike.

49. The seventh warship to carry the name *Weymouth* was a light cruiser, built at the Elswick Shipyards, Newcastle, and completed in 1911. During the First World War it saw action at the Rufiji River in East Africa in 1915, and survived to serve in the peacetime navy of the 1920's. Placed on the disposal list in 1927, H.M.W. *Weymouth* was finally sold for breaking up on 2nd October 1928. A crest from the ship was presented to the town and is displayed in Weymouth Museum, whilst the ship's silver, presented by the Weymouth Corporation on 13th November 1911, has survived and is at present on show at H.M.S. *Collingwood,* the Naval Weapons Engineering School at Fareham, waiting for a future ship of the same name. The photograph shows the cruiser at anchor off Bincleaves with the Nothe Fort in the background.

50. At the southern end of the Nothe Gardens is a site known as The Lookout. The origin of the name is obvious, this being the nearest position to the Weymouth harbour area where it was possible to look out to the sea and observe ships approaching from the east or from around the Island of Portland. The postcard, dating from about 1925, shows a link with Georgian Weymouth – the cabin from a bathing machine in use as a summer house in a garden close to The Lookout. This was not the Royal Bathing Machine which is now restored and on display in Weymouth Museum, although the 'Royal' machine did occupy a place in the same garden many years ago, prior to being dismantled and placed in store.

51. The walk along the coast between the Nothe Gardens and Sandsfoot Cove has been popular with both residents and visitors alike since the early 1890's. Unfortunately, the cliffs have been subject to erosion and collapse, and 'Under Barn Walk' has been damaged and diverted on numerous occasions. The construction of Portland breakwaters during the nineteenth century increased the rate of coastal erosion rather than the reverse, and the past hundred years has seen the disappearance of the sandy foreshore along this stretch of coast, as well as the undermining of the cliffs. The 'Barn' of 'Under Barn' was the old 'Folly Barn' which once stood a little way back from the cliff top and is commemorated today by the name of a house in Belle Vue Road.

52. A victim of coastal erosion on the shoreline of Portland Harbour has been the Tudor castle at Sandsfoot. Erected as part of a general scheme of fortification for the south coast of England during the reign of King Henry VIII, the Castle, together with its companion fortification of Portland Castle, was designed to protect Portland roads against pirates and French raiders. It fell into early disuse and has been a picturesque ruin for the past two hundred years. It was purchased by the Weymouth Corporation in 1902 and the surrounding land laid out as Public Gardens in the 1930's, designed to match the period of the ruin. This photograph of 1903 shows a large portion of the ruin overhanging the cliff, and this section did eventually fall away during the 1950's.

53. At the time of this photograph, about 1905, it was a regular practice for the Channel Island steamers to be turned in harbour to enable them to sail again bow first. Today, the greatly increased size of the ships prevents this manoeuvre, and the ferries normally leave the port stern first. The landing stage and passenger facilities on the pier had been erected in 1888-89, but there was no further reclamation of land until the building of the Pavilion Theatre in 1908. The pier was rebuilt and extended in 1933, and today major reclamations from the sea have completely altered the harbourside area which is depicted here.

54. The paddle steamer *Empress* shown here loaded with holidaymakers and ready to sail from Weymouth pier, was part of the local holiday scene for over 75 years, a period which included service with the Royal Navy in two world wars. Purchased new in 1879, the *Empress* was a comparatively small vessel of only 173 tons gross, but was very popular with several generations of summer visitors. In her later years her main excursions were to Lulworth Cove and around Portland Harbour, and she was finally sold for scrap at the end of the 1955 season. Her set of oscillating engines has been preserved in the Southampton Maritime Museum.

55. The last properties in Weymouth which actually backed onto the harbour stood at the end of Hope Street, and survived until 1888. This group of old cotttages and stores was demolished to enable the Cove to be enlarged and to permit the handling of larger cross-channel vessels being brought to Weymouth by the Great Western Railway, which had just taken over the operation of the service from the Weymouth and Channel Islands Steam Packet Company. Land behind the Cove itself had been reclaimed in 1781, prior to which the harbour reached up as far as what we now know as Hope Square.

56. The enlarged Cove on the southern side of Weymouth Harbour provided good moorings for the Great Western Railway vessels temporarily out of use, and here we see the *Reindeer* with the smaller *Lynx* moored alongside her. The sailing ship on the Melcombe side is typical of those which traded into Weymouth from the Baltic ports until well into the present century and it is moored adjacent to the old Fish Market on Custom House Quay. The Fish Market was built in 1855, but was used for this purpose for just over a decade, when the trade was transferred to the general Market House in St. Mary Street. The Fish Market was then used for general harbour storage, a function it still carries out today. The paddle steamer is the *Albert Victor,* which served at Weymouth from 1889 to 1928 as a pleasure steamer, tug and naval liberty boat, according to the needs of the moment. The picture dates from about 1900.

57. What appears at first glance to be a warship belonging to the Nelson era, was in fact a former convict ship *Success,* at one time used as a prison hulk in Australia. Her visit to Weymouth in 1904 was part of a tour of coastal towns and ports, where visitors could pay to inspect the vessel and wonder at the harsh conditions of this type of imprisonment. The ship was a popular attraction for visitors and must have been a good investment for the firm operating her. This photograph also gives a good idea of the narrow central opening of the Town Bridge – the only place where the bridge could be opened to permit the passage of vessels. The bridge survived until 1928, when it was replaced by the present one.

58. This view of 1898, taken from the Wyke Road, gives a good idea of the way in which the town of Weymouth had spread into the area of Westham during the latter years of the nineteenth century. The first bridge across the Backwater was not built until 1859 and survived until 1921. The first permanent house to be built in Westham dates from 1880 and the eighteen years between that date and the taking of this photograph saw the construction of all of the housing shown to the left of the railway embankment. The embankment itself dates from the early 1860's, when the railway line to Portland was constructed and carried the track across Weymouth Marsh, and area hitherto open to the harbour. The Backwater of 1898 was considerably wider than it is today, extensive reclamations having taken place subsequently on both the Melcombe and Westham sides.

59. The wooden bridge built across the Backwater in 1859 is shown to much better advantage in this view taken about 1885. The drawbridges in the centre were removed in 1888, although the Weymouth Corporation had tried hard to keep the navigation of the River Wey open. The dam in the foreground was built in 1872 to control the flow of the Backwater and to maintain a reasonable level of water in Radipole Lake. The exposed mud in the upper reaches of the lake often smelt somewhat objectionable, and if necessary the retained water could be released to flush out the lower reaches of the harbour. The New Bridge Inn on the far side of the picture was named after the first bridge of 1859 and not its present-day successor which followed in 1921.

60. Following the completion of the new Westham Bridge in 1921, a start was made on the reclamation from Radipole Lake of a strip of land between the new bridge and Melcombe Regis Station. By the time this photograph was taken the work had been completed and the new embankment wall along the far side of Radipole Park Drive can be seen on the left, on the far side of Radipole Lake. Melcombe Regis Boys School on the opposite side of the bridge was built on reclaimed land and opened in 1911. It became Weymouth's Local History Museum in 1971. Reclaimed land in the foreground, on either side of Abbotsbury Road, provided sites for the Health Centre and Central Library, developments which did not follow for some years.

61. When the railway to Portland first opened in 1865 it crossed the Backwater by means of a wooden bridge, which had been completed three years earlier. In 1909 this bridge was replaced by an iron viaduct, built alongside and to the north of the original structure, and in this photograph the two can be seen together. The new viaduct is being tested by four tank engines crossing at the same time, and shortly afterwards the old wooden bridge was removed. The new bridge was considerably shorter than the old, permanent embankments having been constructed out from each side of the lake. The end of one of these can be seen on the right-hand side of the picture.

62. The lengthy embankment built out from the Westham side of Radipole Lake, in order to shorten the new iron railway viaduct, can be seen to better advantage in this postcard of 1913. The brick archway at the extreme left of the picture was constructed to permit the free flow of the lake, but it was better known to modern Weymouthians as the entrance to the Westham Car Parks and the Funfair. The lake of 1913 was very much wider than it is today. Infilling on the Melcombe side had already begun when this photograph was taken, and subsequent reclamations on the Westham side, nearest the camera, have resulted in the modern shoreline which is just beyond the far end of the embankment.

63. The building of a quay wall along the length of Commercial Road had commenced at the end of the eighteenth century and was completed in the early 1860's, in time for the construction of the railway line leading from Weymouth Station to the harbour. The small branch line, or 'tramway' as it was generally known, was brought into use in 1865 and the terraces of houses at the northern end of Commercial Road all date from that period. When first constructed, and until the 1920's, these houses looked out directly onto the Backwater, or Radipole Lake as this part is better known today, but between about 1909 and the mid-1920's the area between Melcombe Regis Station and Westham Bridge was filled in as far as the line of modern Radipole Park Drive.

64. Alexandra Terrace, shown here about 1900, had been completed in 1864, and marked the northern limit of Commercial Road. Here the tramway from the harbour crossed the end of King Street and entered the station yards. This same tramway is the modern 'railway through the street' which is such a well-known feature of Weymouth today, and a traffic problem never visualised when it was first laid down along the newly completed quay wall.

65. No records exist as to when the swans first colonised the Weymouth Backwater and Radipole Lake, but they have been an accepted feature for many years. In this view they can be seen collecting food alongside the quay wall between Melcombe Regis Station and Westham Bridge, an area which has now been filled in, and which today forms Melcombe Regis Gardens. In recent years the numbers of swans have declined drastically, and although popular with both residents and visitors, it is unlikely that the Radipole Lake of the late-twentieth century will ever support the large numbers of swans known to older generations of Weymouthians.

66. Following the completion of the iron railway viaduct across Radipole Lake, a new station to serve the Portland Branch was built on land which had been reclaimed at the northern end of the new bridge. Known as Melcombe Regis Station, it opened on 30th May 1909, and from then on passengers changing from the main line at Weymouth Station were required to walk the short distance along King Street to the new departure point. For the previous 44 years the Portland trains had left from the main Weymouth Station, a far more convenient procedure for the traveller, who was unlikely to have welcomed this 'improvement'. The photograph shows the first of the infilling which when completed was to be laid out as Melcombe Regis Gardens, but which today lies beneath the road improvements at the western end of King Street.

67. The newly reclaimed area north of Westham Bridge was used for a variety of purposes whilst it was allowed to settle, and was a temporary home for travelling fairs and menageries. The helter-skelter shown here about 1922, was later to be a regular summer attraction on Weymouth sands and is shown in another of this selection of old postcards. Another feature of nineteenth century Weymouth, the old wood-pond, was also filled in as part of these reclamations. It occupied the area between the helter-skelter and the shed on the right-hand side of the photograph.

68. On the skyline a train climbs the high embankment constructed in the early 1860's to carry the Weymouth and Portland railway to Rodwell and Wyke Regis, where it crossed the water at Smallmouth by way of a viaduct. Opened in 1865, the railway closed one hundred years later, although it ceased to carry passengers in 1952. The large buildings to the right of this 1930's photograph were the retort houses of Weymouth gasworks. These became obsolete when gas ceased to be manufactured in Weymouth and were demolished in 1962. Westwey House, a block of government offices, now fills the site. Westwey Road, along the western shore of the Backwater, was not completed until as late as 1932. Today, much of the large expanse of water shown here is occupied by pontoon moorings for the hundreds of small pleasure craft which use Weymouth harbour as their base.

69. North Quay, on the Weymouth side of the harbour, in about 1925, a scene which has changed completely today. All the buildings on the right-hand side of the photograph were cleared away in the early 1960's and the site is now occupied by the Municipal Offices and its car parks. The roadway itself is the result of nineteenth century reclamations. In previous centuries the buildings had looked out directly onto the harbour, separated from the water by only a narrow pathway along the old quay wall. The Tudor House, No. 4 North Quay, can be seen in the centre of the photograph. In the background is the Town Bridge, altered in 1880-81, and replaced by the present bridge just a few years after this picture was taken.

70. No. 4 North Quay, Weymouth's Tudor House, photographed in the early 1900's. This was a fine example of a late sixteenth century town house, and was probably the residence of the harbourmaster, with its first floor windows positioned to give a good view of shipping passing up and down the harbour. Strenuous efforts by local conservationists failed to save the building when the site west of the Town Bridge was scheduled for redevelopment in the 1960's. No. 4 was pulled down together with all the old North Quay properties which faced onto the harbour. This postcard bears the caption 'No. 4. North Quay in 'Will Hewling" – a reference to its use as a location in a novel by Alice Hall, a Weymouth author at the turn of the century.

71. In the days long before the development of the eighteenth century seaside resort, two small rival ports had grown up at the mouth of the River Wey – Melcombe on the north side of the harbour and Weymouth on the south side. Building land close to the harbour on the Weymouth side was restricted by the high ground of Chapelhay and resulted in the pattern of densely-packed houses clustered along the river bank. The narrow street which once ran close behind the buildings on North Quay can be seen here – High Street, which was a continuation of the road in front of the old Town Hall. Cleared in the early 1960's, these properties made way for Municipal Offices, opened in 1971 by Her Royal Highness Princess Anne in celebration of the 400th anniversary of the Union by charter dated 1st June 1571 of the once rival towns of Weymouth and Melcombe Regis into one Borough.

72. High West Street, Weymouth, at its junction with Boot Hill, photographed in about 1910. The end wall of the little shop on the corner (a barber's, complete with the traditional striped pole outside) bears a variety of posters advertising goods ranging from starch to shoes, and pianos to prams, and entertainments such as the circus, football match, swimming club meeting, concert and 'Review of Reviews'. The buildings on the right-hand side are recognisable today, and Weymouth's 'Old Town Hall' is little changed. The houses on the left, however, were all demolished in the 1930's to provide the site for Weymouth's Fire Station, previously situated in cramped accommodation in St. Edmund Street. The terraces of houses which were pulled down were Jockey's Row, Silver Street and West Plains.

73. Edwardsville near the top of Rodwell Avenue was built in 1896 to provide homes for twenty of the aged poor of Weymouth. It was the gift of Sir Henry Edwards, M.P. for Weymouth for some twenty years in the latter half of the nineteenth century. His great concern for the poor in the town he represented was manifested in a number of charitable actions, and the year before Edwardsville was built, Sir Henry had paid for the erection of ten cottage homes at Edwards Avenue, Boot Hill. His annual dinner for those of three score years and upwards had been started in the 1870's, whilst other projects funded by him included the Working Men's Club in Mitchell Street, the mechanism and illumination of the Jubilee Clock, and a set of bells for Christchurch. He also donated a handsome clock for the front of the Old Town Hall during its restoration in the 1890's.

74. This Tudor building stands in Trinity Street on the south side of the harbour. It was once the home of Thomas Geiar, a wealthy merchant and sometime Mayor and M.P. of Weymouth in the seventeenth century. In the mid-1700's as the town began to develop as a resort, the building housed the first Assembly Rooms, providing entertainment for the new visitors. Soon though, the Melcombe side of the harbour became the centre of the seaside industry and new Assembly Rooms opened on the Esplanade. These original rooms in less fashionable Weymouth lost their popularity and became known as the Old Rooms, the name the building has kept to the present day. It is now used as an office by the local firm of Devenish Weymouth Breweries Ltd.

75. The whole of Chapelhay suffered very serious damage and heavy casualties in Second World War air raids during 1940 and 1941. The terraced houses shown here in Oakley Place were demolished in a night raid on 9th May 1941. The photograph dates from happier times and shows the street decked with flags to celebrate the Coronation of King Edward VII in 1902. Many of the old place names in this area were lost following the clearance of damaged properties after the war – Queen's Place, Southampton Row, Havelock Place and others, have now disappeared. Chapelhay itself takes its name from the mediaeval chapel of St. Nicholas which stood on this high ground above Weymouth and was destroyed during Civil War fighting in the 1640's.

76. When first consecrated in 1836, Holy Trinity Church occupied a very narrow site in High Street (now known as Trinity Road) and houses crowded right up to its walls on either side. In the 1880's it was decided to improve access to Chapelhay by the construction of a new road, and properties on the west side of Holy Trinity were demolished for this purpose. Plans for the road were later abandoned and the scheme carried out was one of flights of steps with connecting slopes, some of which are shown in this photograph. At the same time the church was greatly enlarged by the addition of the large new transept on the western side of the nave. The other buildings have changed little in the eighty years since this postcard was published, apart from the Town Bridge which was taken down and replaced during 1928-1930.

77. This street scene of the early 1880's is not so different from that of today, although there had been changes in St. Edmund Street earlier in the nineteenth century. The porticoed Guildhall opened in 1838 and replaced earlier town halls on the same site. Facing down the street, Maiden Street Methodist Church was built in the 1860's where an old coaching inn, The King's Head, had once stood. In Georgian times, mail coaches for London, Bath and the West of England had left from the Golden Lion Inn (centre left). Outside the bow-fronted building in the left foreground (then owned by James Robertson, dealer in household goods and one-time Mayor of Weymouth) stands one of the bath chairs used to transport the frail and elderly around the town. The building on the corner of St. Mary Street and St. Edmund Street was owned by grocer R.J. Wright, and was known as 'Wright's English Naples Stores', Weymouth at that time advertising itself as 'The Naples of England'.

78. The lower end of St. Mary Street, looking north, in the early years of this century. The buildings in the foreground on the right-hand side of the picture have all been altered since this photograph was taken. Adjacent to the church, on the south side, had stood, until its demolition in the 1880's, a house which dated from the fifteenth century. Some details from it have been incorporated into the present building on the site, No. 45 St. Mary Street. St. Mary's, the parish church of Melcombe Regis, dates from 1817. Beyond it, in this main shopping street of Weymouth, can be seen the ornate façade of the large Market House, designed in the 1850's. The narrowness of St. Mary Street has always been a problem and even in the days before the motor car there must have been congestion here, as handcarts, horse-drawn carts, horse buses and bicycles crowded the roadway.

79. The Market House, St. Mary Street, about 1905. Several dogs wait outside, no doubt lured by enticing smells from the butchers' stalls within. This large and costly building opened in 1855 and was designed by the noted Victorian architect Talbot Bury. Initially it was unpopular with the traders, who found the interior badly arranged and their stallholders' rents too high! In this century, the use of the Market House declined and in 1939 the decision was taken to pull it down. Today, with the popularity of markets generally and the building's central position, it would undoubtedly have been an asset to the town. Only one wall was left standing (seen here covered in ivy) and this now forms part of the modern Market House – in fact a row of shops with a central passage leading to Maiden Street.

80. Two passengers make the perilous ascent of the steps leading to the top deck of a horse-drawn bus outside the Golden Lion Inn in St. Mary Street, around the turn of the century. A second horse-drawn bus approaches down the street – motor buses were not seen in Weymouth until 1905. Passers-by gaze in the windows of Mr. Wright's grocery store offering goods 'of the choicest quality at the lowest possible prices'. Beyond was another grocer, Gosden's Cash Store.

81. St. Mary Street in the early 1890's, seen at its junction with St. Alban Street. With many buildings in the town centre only the shopfronts have altered over the years, but this is not the case at No. 71, Acutt's Refreshment Rooms, shown in the foreground on the right of the picture. In complete contrast to the plain bow-windowed buildings shown here, this corner site was completely rebuilt in 1898, in a highly decorative style, and the first floor can still be seen today. Opposite, Albion House still bears its name at first-floor level, although many businesses have occupied its ground floor (Curry's store today). Talbot the draper was there in 1890, advertising his 'millinery, mantle, costume, carpet and linoleum showrooms'. Victorian children pose somewhat self-consciously in the foreground.

82. St. Mary Street, photographed from its junction with Bond Street, looking north, in the early 1900's. V.H. Bennett was eventually to acquire Nos. 88, James Morris, bootmaker, 89, Lovell's creamery and 90, Garratt Jones, outfitter, to extend his department store in the two main streets. Taken over by Debenhams until 1982, this is now the site of John Menzies store. On the opposite side of the street, the buildings shown were demolished in 1923 to make way for Woolworth's first Weymouth store, subsequently greatly enlarged. Further up the street on the same side, out of sight in this picture, more old properties disappeared when Marks and Spencer built the first part of their store in the early 1930's. The tall Lloyds Bank building (centre left) had replaced an umbrella shop by the time this photograph was taken – it was then the premises of the Wilts and Dorset Bank.

83. An earlier photograph of St. Mary Street, probably dating from the 1870's. The tiny shop which housed Russell the umbrella maker and repairer, disappeared in the early 1880's and on this site now stands the Lloyds Bank building. Note the delightful umbrella sign which surmounts the fascia board above the window of No. 92. Further up the street at this date were the premises of Samuel Chick, the Honiton lace manufacturer (No. 100), Miss Collis, the dress and mantle maker (No. 97) and Mrs. Hassell's fancy repository. At the top of the street, not shown here, were the Royal Baths, built in the early 1840's and demolished in 1927.

84. The cannon ball, lodged in the wall of the ancient house on the corner of Maiden Street and St. Edmund Street, is Weymouth's traditional link with the fighting of the Civil War. In February 1645, it was almost certainly fired as part of the bombardment of Melcombe Regis by Royalist forces operating from the temporary fort on the Nothe headland, during the most violent period of conflict of the whole of the war in this area. The incident of the cannon ball is not recorded or documented in any way, but local tradition is strong, and the date quoted is a logical one. The old house carrying the cannon ball has been restored and is still very much a period structure, but the attractive old Tudor dwellings on the opposite corner were demolished many years ago and replaced by shop premises.

85. A typical old family business was that of Cornick Bros., bakers, founded in Governor's Lane towards the end of the last century. In these early days, bread, cakes and buns were sold from baskets around the town and on the sands, but with the purchase of this shop, Cornicks were able to extend their trade to include groceries and provisions. The shop stood on the corner of East Street and Governor's Lane and is today devoted to the sale of antiques. The central figure in the group is William Cornick, who with his elder brother John had founded the firm. They had learned much of their trade from their father, Tom Cornick, the older figure on the left of the group. This shop was sold about 1908 and the business was then concentrated at the Dorchester Road premises, indicated above the doorway.

86. This distant view of Weymouth Station as seen along Park Street was a familiar sight from the opening of the railway service in 1857, until the early 1950's when the great overall station roof was removed. The station had been a good example of Brunel's designs for the Great Western Railway, but the roof was its essential feature, and with this gone the remaining buildings lost their unity and the majority have now been removed. Christchurch, the tower of which is such an imposing feature of this view, was erected in 1874 as a Chapel of Ease to St. Mary's Church, but closed in 1939 and was finally demolished in 1956-57.

87. The buildings on the departure side of Weymouth station were still in reasonable condition in July 1923, when His Royal Highness The Prince of Wales visited the town. He is shown here arriving at the station in the company of the Mayor of Weymouth (Councillor W.J. Gregory), after a brief afternoon visit. He had lunched at Dorchester with Thomas Hardy, and then, following a visit to Upwey Wishing Well, arrived at the King's Statue to be welcomed by the Mayor and Corporation and the assembled townsfolk. After tea at the Gloucester Hotel, he left by the 5.20 p.m. train.

88. This crowded scene at Weymouth Station during the summer of 1924 marked the beginning of a three day trip to the British Empire Exhibition at Wembley, by 260 Weymouth schoolchildren and their teachers. The party was away from Tuesday morning to Thursday evening. The extensive accommodation at Weymouth Station is obvious from this view, and included six platforms plus storage sidings. Most of the railway carriages shown here were of Great Western stock, including many of the well-known 'clerestories'.

89. Much of the land behind the houses which fronted onto Weymouth Esplanade was recovered from the Backwater as part of a major scheme of reclamation which commenced in 1834. Originally intended for use as a park, the land was never raised high enough, and when at a later date plans were changed and the land sold for building, inadequate drainage was one of the constant problems of this area of the town. Somewhat more serious than usual was the flooding of October 1908, when, following heavy rainfall, several streets were under water. A special pumping system has been installed to deal with this problem and floods as serious as this are now a thing of the past.

90. The return of troops at the end of the Boer War was the cause of great celebration, and here we see a contingent of the Dorset Yeomanry being welcomed as they marched up King Street away from Weymouth Station. We are uncertain as to the identity of the group of civilians heading the procession, but they are followed by choir boys, and in the distance, beneath the welcoming sign, can be seen the victorious troops. Twelve Weymouth men who had served in the war were granted the Freedom of the Borough in 1900. The Sun Public House on the corner of Crescent Street has been completely rebuilt since this view of over eighty years ago.

91. The 1920's saw great changes in public transport at Weymouth, and this scene, shortly after lunch on a summer afternoon, shows the char-a-bancs loading up for their tours to local beauty spots. The National Bus Company had not yet arrived on the scene, and local transport was in the hands of smaller units such as the Weymouth Motor Company and a number of private owners. One horse-drawn waggonette still plies for hire, although this type of transport was soon to become very much a novelty. Apart from the erection of a large bus shelter adjoining the King's Statue, the area retained its open aspect until the creation of the Statue Gardens in 1956 and the introduction of a one-way traffic system.

92. Until 1895, the top of Lodmoor Hill, shown in this photograph, marked the northern boundary of the Borough of Weymouth and Melcombe Regis. Today this is one of the two busiest main roads leading into Weymouth, and most of the domestic buildings shown here have been replaced by shops. This is the principal commercial area serving the day-by-day-needs of the extensive housing estates which have grown up at the back of the main Dorchester Road, development which began in the mid- and late-Victorian era and saw further rapid growth in both the 1920's and 1930's.

93. By 1925, the main road from Weymouth over Lodmoor Hill and on towards Dorchester, was accustomed to the steady flow of motor vehicles, having seen a regular service of double-decker buses since the pioneer days of 1905. Here such a bus hugs the crown of the road to avoid the top-deck passengers being injured by the luxuriant growth of the avenue of trees lining the route. Prior to 1895 this area had been in the Parish of Radipole, and much of the development here had taken place before it became part of the Borough of Weymouth and Melcombe Regis.

94. The origin of the custom of 'Beating the Bounds' goes back to the days when maps were few and vague, and it was essential that as many residents as possible were fully aware of the position of the Borough boundaries. The custom has been carried out at Weymouth on a number of occasions, but not on a regular annual or 'multi-year' pattern. This postcard records a visit to one of the boundary stones during the 'beating' ceremony carried out in 1909, when a local schoolboy was being bumped on the stone in order to impress on his 'memory' the exact location of this point on the Borough boundary. School-children have often taken an active part in these ceremonies, and in the 1933 perambulation which marked the expansion of the Borough to include Upwey, Broadwey, Radipole, Preston and Wyke Regis, every school in the new Borough took part. The ceremony was repeated fifty years later in 1983.

95. Built in the closing years of the last century, Spa View Terrace, Radipole, was one of the earliest developments on the land facing the site of the old Spa. The Congregational Church at the far end of the Terrace was opened in 1905 and completely rebuilt during the years 1953-54. This photograph dates from about 1910 and proves that not every view changes drastically with the passage of time. Every house in the terrace was named after a particular specie of tree, with the names carved into the stone lintels of each property.

96. A popular subject with postcard publishers from the earliest days has been the northern shore of Radipole Lake in the vicinity of St. Ann's Church. This view dates from about 1910, and is in fact a rather badly re-touched photograph. Today, many of the trees have gone and the whole scene is much more open, whilst what was then a definite 'shoreline' is today a somewhat overgrown river, resulting from the general silting up which followed the construction of the Westham Embankment Bridge in 1921. Radipole is a traditional landing site for galleys when the Roman town of Durnovaria (Dorchester) was being founded, but whilst this suggestion is quite logical, changes in the landscape during the past 2,000 years have obliterated any definite evidence of a Roman port.

97. When this photograph was taken, about 1910, the Parish Church of Radipole was still dedicated to St. Mary. Administratively it had been a Chapel of Ease to St. Mary's Church, Melcombe Regis since 1606, but in 1927 it was once again to revert to full Parish Church status and to be re-dedicated to St. Ann. The church dates largely from the thirteenth century, whilst the adjoining building, known today as The Old Manor House, Radipole, is of sixteenth century origin. The scene is little changed today.

98. The degree to which the upper parts of Radipole Lake have silted up during the past fifty years is shown by studying this view taken about 1910. In those days the river was tidal as far as Radipole, although the dam across the Backwater at Westham did control the level of water in the lake to a major degree. The new Westham Bridge of 1921 provided complete control over the waters of the River Wey, and since then what in this photograph were clearly mudflats with some vegetation, are today well-established fields, abutting onto a very much narrowed River Wey, but still subject to flooding at certain periods of the year. The worst flooding ever occurred on the night of 18th/19th July 1955, when a record 11 inches of rain fell in one night on the hills above Portesham and the following day the floods hit the valley of the River Wey!

99. A winter's scene at the north end of Radipole Lake during the early years of this century. Abbots Court, the large house on the skyline to the left of the picture, had been completed in 1897 by John Baggs, builder and one time Mayor of Weymouth. Eventually the road adjoining was developed as Ullswater Crescent and in the mid-1920's a new road was constructed from Radipole southwards across the lake, and is known today as Radipole Park Drive. Almost all the lake visible in this picture has been reclaimed by the process of pumping silt from the remainder of the lake across the new Park Drive and then allowing it to settle. Here today are the playing fields adjoining the railway line.

100. Active hunting within the Borough boundaries is now virtually a thing of the past, but this was far from the case back in about 1900 when this photograph was taken at Corfe Hill House, Radipole. It was the home of Squire Thresher, who was acting as host to the Cattistock Hunt. Today Corfe Hill House had been converted into flats, and although the parklands surrounding it remained largely undeveloped until the 1970's, they have now succumbed to the spread of modern housing estates.

101. Looking back along the Dorchester Road at Broadwey, this view taken in the early 1920's shows a main road narrower than that of today. The trees and buildings on the left-hand side of the road have now disappeared and houses have been built in this vicinity. Broadwey Farm, on the right, still stands, but looks quite different today. The thatch shown here has been removed and replaced by a tiled roof. Later again the seventeenth century farmhouse was restored to its original appearance by the removal of the bay-windowed extension which in the twenties fronted directly onto the street. In the distance a cart is standing at the turning to Littlemead.

102. The Dorchester Road at Broadwey once again, this time looking north, in the early 1930's. By this date the roof of Broadwey Farm had been tiled and can be seen in the background on the left. Its barn, in the centre of the picture, has been converted more recently, and is now an attractive house. The other buildings on the left are little changed today. The Upwey to Portland bus, an A.E.C. Regent, new in 1929, is forced to keep to the centre of this narrow stretch of road, widened later by the removal of the walls and buildings on the right-hand side. Of the settlements along the River Wey, the 'Waia' of Domesday, it was the village of Broadwey which clung longest to the alternative spelling of 'Broadway', Upwey and Weymouth having adopted the more usual form of 'Wey'.

103. Broadwey Mill, photographed in the late nineteenth century, with the workforce posed in front of, and leaning out of, the building. Adjacent to the Mill stands Mill House built in the 1850's. The mill itself is of earlier date but it was considerably enlarged in the early-Victorian period. In the present century a timber bridge was built high above Mill Street to link the mill with associated buildings opposite. The mill buildings which survive along the River Wey are well cared for and a striking reminder of an age when water power from the local river provided industry and employment in the villages of Radipole, Nottington, Broadwey and Upwey (where the mill in Church Street is still in use).

104. The octagonal three-story Spa House at Nottington was built in 1830 to the designs of Robert Vining, a local architect/builder who had worked with James Hamilton on the Esplanade terraces and other Georgian buildings in the town. The health giving properties of the waters at Nottington had been recognised long before this date and in the eighteenth century John Crane had published his 'Account of the nature, properties and medicinal uses of the mineral water at Nottington, near Weymouth, Dorset'. The first guidebook of Weymouth in 1785, whilst advocating the new fashion for sea bathing as a cure for practically all known medical conditions, also devoted several pages to the benefits to be gained from sampling the mineral water at Nottington, recognisable by 'the brisk smell of sulphur it copiously emits'.

105. Upwey, at the head of the River Wey, was known until the thirteenth century as 'Way Bayouse', the Lords of the Manor in early times being the family of Bayouse, from Bayeux in Normandy. John Bayouse founded a little chantry here in 1244 and it could be from this that the Church of St. Lawrence evolved. Beyond the village rises Gould's Hill, the road shown climbing across the Ridgeway to Winterborne St. Martin (Martinstown). John Leland, the Tudor antiquarian, passed through Upwey in the course of his travels in 1538. In his record known as Leland's Itinerary, he described his visit: *From Frampton to Upwey, all by hilly ground, barren of wood exceeding good for sheep, a four miles. At this Upwey, at the right-hand as I came in is the very head of the Wey River, that of some is called 'Wile'.* Leland is the only historian who has referred to the river by this alternative name of 'Wile'.

106. The exact date when the springs at Upwey became known as Upwey Wishing Well is uncertain. The name was used in 'Broken Bonds', a locally-set romantic adventure novel by Hawley Smart, and Upwey Wishing Well may date from the publication of the book in 1874. This stone shelter at the well was erected in 1905 and the initials G.T.I.G. are those of a member of the Gould family, owners of the site for many years. Prior to this, a wooden shelter had stood on the same spot. It is the custom to sip the well water, make a wish and toss the remaining contents of the glass over the left shoulder back into the well. This traditional ceremony was observed by His Royal Highness The Prince of Wales (later King Edward VIII), in July 1923, when he visited Upwey, the village which often welcomed his great-great-great-grandfather, King George III in the days of 'Royal Weymouth', 1789-1805.

107. Trips by horse-drawn char-a-bancs to local beauty spots were popular with visitors in the first quarter of this century. Mr. Jesty's four-in-hand coach 'Vivid' started out from the King's Statue and the ride ended here at Upwey Wishing Well. Before the return journey a strawberry tea and ice cream could be enjoyed at Tom English's refreshment room adjacent to the well. In the background stand the Victorian buildings of the village school. Upwey School closed in 1976, but these premises are still an important centre of community life in their modern role of Village Hall.

108. The Dorchester Road at Upwey. The tinker's caravan in the background will shortly begin the climb to the hairpin bend on the Ridgeway. The public house on the right, The Royal Oak, was demolished in 1968 to improve traffic visibility on this corner at the bottom of the hill. Leading straight up the Ridgeway opposite is the steep Old Roman Road to Dorchester. The county town is now reached by the main road, cut in the 1820's, which follows the contours of the hill but still presents problems at the acutely-angled hairpin bend at its junction with the turning to Bincombe.

109. As with the other villages around Weymouth, Preston did not become part of the Borough until 1933. Since 1812, the main road eastwards out of Weymouth has run through the centre of the village of Preston, bridging the River Jordan just beyond where the policeman is shown cycling on patrol. Increased traffic, and the development of huge holiday camps in the vicinity of this village have had a major effect on the economy and much of the rural atmosphere, so much a part of this view, has given way to road improvements and modern housing.

110. The rural atmosphere of the village of Preston is even more obvious in this detailed view of the area to the left of the previous picture. Being off the main road this has not changed to quite the same degree. The ancient footbridge, known locally as 'The Roman Bridge', still exists today, and although modern buildings have been interspersed with the old, the scene is easily recognised.

111. As the main road through Preston leaves the village to start its long climb over Osmington Hill, it passes the Ship Inn and the road leading to the neighbouring village of Sutton Poyntz. When this view was taken about 1910, the road was very narrow at this point, and in recent years the whole of the property on the left of the picture has been swept away to enable the road to be widened and the corner improved. The old cottages adjoining the inn have all been modernised and restored but retain much of their original character, although just off the picture to the right, shops have either been built or converted to serve the needs of the community.

112. The village of Sutton Poyntz, centred around its mill-pond, has altered very little since this photograph was taken some seventy years ago. Water has been drawn from here since 1855 to serve the needs of Weymouth, and the tall chimney in the distance marks the pumping station of the Weymouth Waterworks Company. This chimney has now been demolished, virtually the only change which has taken place in the buildings, and although the large tree has also gone, those which have replaced it have already reached maturity. The water is now pumped by electricity, the hotel has been modernised and undoubtedly the interiors of the houses and cottages would show similar changes, but externally the scene remains constant.

113. A disastrous fire broke out in the village of Sutton Poyntz on the afternoon of Saturday, 18th April 1908. The whole village turned out to fight the flames and to try and salvage some of the contents of the burning cottages, but by the time the Weymouth Fire Brigade arrived, nearly a quarter of a mile of buildings was on fire. The Brigade managed to contain the fire to one side of the road, but the destruction amounted to several thousands of pounds. The Court House, opposite the Mill, was completely destroyed in the fire and in spite of the efforts of the local residents, several farm animals were lost in the blaze. The Fire Brigade was on duty from 3.00 p.m. on the Saturday afternoon until 9.00 a.m. on the Sunday, and was recalled on the Monday to deal with a further outbreak.

114. The Old Mill at Sutton Poyntz, no longer required for the purpose for which it was designed, has recently been restored and a residential flat constructed within the building. Future plans include the landscaping of the mill leet and the restoration of the waterwheel and milling machinery. This photograph was probably taken about 1905 before the fire which destroyed and damaged so much of the village. The Old Court House immediately opposite the mill, where once a year the inhabitants of Sutton Poyntz were required to pay there ground rents to the Weld Estate, has gone. Those buildings of Northdown Farm, beyond the Court House, which had to be replaced after the fire, have long since weathered and become part of the village scene.

BOWLEASE BEACH, OVERCOMBE.

115. At the northern end of Weymouth Bay, the small cove at the mouth of the River Jordan remained virtually undeveloped until the 1930's. Prior to 1812 the main road out of Weymouth to the east had led over this hill and then up the Jordan Valley, but in that year it was diverted by way of Chalbury Corner, as it is today. This view dates from the 1920's, since when houses along the length of Overcombe Drive and holiday facilities down near the foreshore have contributed to a major alteration of the scene, whilst off picture to the right, the Riviera Hotel of 1937 represents the largest man-made change to the scene. However, man alone has not been the only cause of changes here. Furzy Cliff in the background of the photograph has always been unstable and in recent years serious falls have resulted in the need to construct vast coast protection schemes from Overcombe Corner along towards Bowleaze Cove.

116. One of the most photographed objects in the Weymouth area is The White Horse, a hill figure carved on the slopes of the hill above Osmington. Intended to portray King George III on his white horse, it was carved in the chalk in the year 1808. The work was directed by a Weymouth bookseller, John Wood, who owned the land on which the figure was carved, the cost being met by John Rainier. From time to time the figure has to be cleared of weeds in an effort to improve its 'whiteness' but although still visible for many miles, the King and his charger are no longer the pristine figures of the early nineteenth century. King George III never saw this tribute to his visits to Weymouth, and the many variations of the legend that he was annoyed because it showed him riding away from Weymouth, have no foundation in truth.

117. The Coastguard Cottages at Overcombe, overlooking Weymouth Bay and Lodmoor, are the centrepiece of this view of about 1925. This part of Lodmoor, perhaps better drained than the rest, has been the scene of horse-racing during the nineteenth century and of commercial flights round the bay in an open cockpit biplane during the 1920's. Housing now covers much of the higher land, although cliff falls, mentioned in the commentary to view No. 115, have resulted in a major part of the Coastguard Cottages slipping over the cliff edge into the sea. Plans for the development of Lodmoor have been numerous and mostly unproductive, and much of the 'moor' remains a slowly diminishing home for wild birds and the controlled disposal of household refuse. The latest scheme for a 'country park' holds promise of a logical development of this area.

118. These Edwardian children are posed outside the small schoolhouse in the Square at Wyke Regis, built in the 1820's by a Dr. Hoby. Here, members of Weymouth Baptist Church ran a Sunday School for the village. The other buildings in the Square are little changed today – the small shop on the corner still serves the residents of the older part of Wyke Regis. There was no real expansion of the village until the end of the nineteenth century and then the development was to the south towards Ferrybridge. More recently there has been a spread of housing to the north in the Lanehouse Rocks Road area and also in the Westhill Road area close to the shores of the Fleet.

119. The corner of Wyke Square and All Saints Road in about 1890. The old Baptist schoolhouse is on the left, whilst opposite stands the parish room where the village school was held until new premises were opened in Victoria Road in 1891. The parish room was pulled down in the early years of this century and replaced on the same site by All Saints Memorial Hall, built in memory of the Reverend George Chamberlaine, Rector of the parish in the early-Victorian period. He was responsible for the building in 1836 of Holy Trinity Church at Weymouth, and also gave his name to Chamberlaine Road at Wyke Regis, on the corner of which the Hall now stands.

120. Around the turn of the century, this photograph was taken of part of Shrubbery Lane, Wyke Regis, close to its junction with Kaye's Lane. The scene is much changed today. The thatched cottage in the background has been replaced by a modern brick house, and all the cottages on the left had to be cleared following severe damage during a Second World War air raid on 28th June 1942. This is part of 'old' Wyke, the ancient village which had developed in very early times close to the shores of the Fleet. The growth of the area along Portland Road between Foord's Corner and Ferrybridge came much later and followed the arrival of industry in Wyke Regis – the Whitehead Torpedo Works built in 1891.

121. Portland Road, Wyke Regis, in the 1920's, at its junction with Williams Avenue. There is still a garage on the site shown here, but J.R. Jones' drapers shop is today a Chinese 'take-away'. Beyond the houses at the top of Williams Avenue stretch open fields – the modern houses on this side of Portland Road were not built until the 1930's. Opposite stand older houses and the Wyke Hotel public house, all these buildings having followed close on the establishment of the Torpedo Works at Ferrybridge. Williams Avenue, Sunnyside Road, Fairview Road, Victoria Road, Gallwey Road and Parkmead Road were all developments of this period. The public gardens which are adjacent to the Wyke Hotel were laid out in the 1930's, one of a number of projects created to provide work for the unemployed.

122. Victoria Road, off the Portland Road at Wyke Regis, is a development of the late nineteenth century and another reminder of the commemoration of Queen Victoria's Diamond Jubilee in 1897. The school, opened in that year, stands at the far end of the road and was built by the Whitehead Torpedo Company, the population of this area having greatly increased following the opening of their new factory. On the right of the photograph, taken in the early 1900's, is the then Wyke Regis Liberal Club, in buildings which now house the Wyke Regis Working Men's Club. Vickers Armstrong later took over the torpedo factory, but since 1971 the engineering company of Wellworthy Ltd. has occupied the premises.

123. One of the more unusual buildings in Wyke Regis is 'Wyke Castle', built in the mid-nineteenth century. It has no military connections whatever, but is simply a private house built to a somewhat unusual design. It stands at the junction of Westhill Road and Pirates Lane. Once it was isolated, but modern housing now stretches down Westhill Road opposite and beyond the castle. The old lane leading down to the Fleet no doubt saw much of the activity of the local 'wreckers' who plundered vessels cast ashore on Chesil Beach. Having rowed their booty across the Fleet to the mainland, these 'salvage experts' would be hastening back to the village via Pirates Lane, having concealed the stolen goods in various hiding places along the shore. Smaller items would be hidden in their homes, well away from the prying eyes of officials sent to retrieve the missing cargo.

124. Whilst the people of the Weymouth area have a long tradition of 'salvaging' goods from vessels wrecked on the Chesil Beach, they have an equally long tradition of life saving at sea, and the final illustration in this selection returns to Weymouth Harbour, where the lifeboat *Friern Watch* makes a considerable splash as it descends the launching ramp from the lifeboat house on Nothe Parade. The first lifeboat was stationed at Weymouth in 1869, and over the years the local lifeboat crews have built up a reputation second to none in successful rescues from ships of all types which have got into difficulty in the dangerous waters off Portland. This photograph dates from about 1910 and shows the original lifeboat house. This was later replaced by a much larger building, but the modern lifeboat remains permanently afloat in the harbour.